Imperfect But Perfectly Made

Lessons Learned in Those Moments
When I Needed God

By: Debra A. Williams

IMPERFECT BUT PERFECTLY MADE

Lessons Learned In Those Moments When I Needed God

DEBRA A. WILLIAMS

ISBN: 979-8-9939574-3-2 (Soft cover), ISBN: 979-8-9939574-4-9 (Hard cover), ISBN: 979-8-9939574-5-6 (E-book)

PRAISE FOR IMPERFECT BUT PERFECTLY MADE

To My Wife, Debra:

As you continue on your faith journey in ministry, may you ever remain sensitive to the leading of God's Spirit. In His time, He will reveal the giftings He has placed in you for the edifying of the body of Christ and His glory. Follow His leading as He takes you from Faith to Faith and Grace to Grace.
Rev. Alan E. Williams

Debra A. Williams's memoir is a moving and hope-filled testimony of what can happen when a believer continually leans into trusting God. With honesty and humility, she invites the reader into her journey of faith, revealing not only moments of struggle, but also the deep spiritual growth and maturation that emerge through perseverance and surrender. Her story is encouraging and relatable, reminding believers that faith is not static but is shaped and strengthened over time as we learn to rely more fully on God's presence, guidance and grace. This memoir stands as a gentle, yet powerful witness to a life transformed through trust in God.
Rev. Dr. Mashona Walston

Debra Williams has written a soul-stirring work that will be a source of inspiration to many. She shares an introspective look at her life's journey. It is a story of triumph over the many pitfalls and challenges one can face in young adulthood. It is the story of how one can beat the odds through perseverance and self-confidence. A great read for girls and young women facing life's challenges.

Dr. Edward O. Williamson
Christian Educator

This book feels less like something to read and more like something to sit while allowing it to speak to our hearts. Through personal revelation and transparency, the writer touches the part of us that loves God deeply, even when we don't feel particularly love-able. It is a timeless and Spirit-lead account that reminds us of God's grace and mercy, and no matter what, we are worthy of His love. What makes this book especially powerful is its honesty. It doesn't pretend that faith erases exhaustion, disappointment, grief, or self-doubt. Instead, it acknowledges the weight we carry— family responsibilities, church expectations, work pressures, and the unspoken belief that we always have to be strong. The author gently pushes back against that lie and reminds us that God never required perfection, only presence. It is that extra push not to quit before the miracle; before the break-through that all women of faith need.

Rev. Dr. Karen Clancy-McMichael

DEDICATION

This Book is dedicated first to God for giving me life, strength, knowledge, courage, wisdom and grace to get this done.

To my husband, Alan, who has had faith in me from day one. He has been my constant and the one I could always depend on. Thank you. Love you, Babe!

My parents, (the late) Willie B. and Virginia Watson, without whom I would not be here. My siblings. My children - Michael, Marcus and Odaysia - and my grands and great grands who will always be the inspiration I need to move forward and upward. Love you all!

"For thou hast possessed my reins: thou hast covered me in my mother's womb. I will praise thee; for I am fearfully and wonderfully made: marvellous are thy works; and that my soul knoweth right well."
- Psalm 139:13-14

CONTENTS

FOREWORD

A person who finds a steadfast friend is blessed. The ability to share and to be vulnerable is a quality not to be taken for granted. I have known Debra as a *sister-friend*, confidante and co-laborer in Christian Education Ministry for a dozen years or so. We are both similar in that we do not aspire to become *fast friends* or claim instant knowledge of anyone upon initial meetings. We both wade in cautiously, surveying, testing the waters, and determining if an acquaintance is trustworthy enough to move from cordial conversation to meaningful engagement.

When Debra and her husband, the Rev. Alan Williams, joined Macedonia Baptist Church in Albany, New York in 2010, I had been laboring with the Sunday School Ministry as a youth teacher for many years. I was thrilled when our pastor at the time tapped Debra to lead the ministry as Sunday School superintendent and bring her extensive Biblical knowledge and Christian education experience to energize our efforts. Eventually, I joined her as an assistant superintendent. We formed an effective team, and over a period of almost 10 years, we alternated between serving as the lead in the ministry and the assistant. Debra tapped her extensive network to organize teacher training workshops and other development opportunities to increase the scope and impact of the ministry. She has consistently, humbly and patiently shared with me and countless others her knowledge and wisdom, not to be in the spotlight, but to help others find their footing in ministry.

I have watched Debra effectively assume leadership roles in both local and state associations, leveraging her vast network with precision, savvy and creativity. I have read her published articles in Christian education journals, listened to her facilitate church leadership workshops, and teach/lecture on a variety of Christian Education topics in our region and at the state level.

I have not been alone in urging Debra to share her experiences and hard-won wisdom in book form. I have been inspired by her perseverance in pursuing an additional advanced degree in Biblical and Educational Studies from Liberty University, while still meeting family commitments and assisting her husband in ministry. Her boundless energy to serve and minister has inspired me to persevere also, and I believe readers of this book will find hope, encouragement and inspiration from the lessons she shares here in navigating life and relationships both inside and outside of the faith community. Debra successfully wears many hats (including actual hats!) - wife to a clergyman, mother and grandmother, student, writer, lecturer, ministry president/chair, Christian education dean/registrar, technology guru, party planner and decorator, fashionista, and sister-friend-comrade in arms!

We have all heard the expression in church circles, *"There is no testimony without a test."* Debra has blessed me and those acquainted with her through friendship and/or ministry by sharing how she has overcome early life challenges, disappointments, and the accompanying grief and discouragement that comes from blown up expectations and plans. As we have prayed with and for each other, celebrated victories and mourned losses, we learned to lean on one of Debra's favorite Scriptures; Jeremiah 29: 11-13 (NIV): *"For I know the plans I have for you," declares the LORD, "plans to prosper you and not to harm you, plans to give you hope and a future. Then you will call on me and come and pray to me, and I will listen to you. You will seek me and find me when you seek me with all your heart."*

I am convinced these lessons shared by Debra will lighten your heart and lead each of you to also lean evermore on God's faithful promises.

Sharon B. Bowles, Esq., Clifton Park, NY

INTRODUCTION

Dear Heavenly Father, please touch my heart, mind and spirit to be open to what you have for me to share. Empower me with the words that I put on these pages, strengthen the hearts that they touch and the lives that they change. In Jesus' name I pray. Amen.

God has placed in me the gifts of encouragement and compassion, which is quite interesting because there have been so many times in my life that I actually was the one who needed the encouragement. I realize now that if I did not go through those situations, I could not encourage or have real compassion for others who are going through tough times.

Before I got serious about my salvation, I went to church regularly. I was involved in different auxiliaries, sang in the choir, and gave faithfully. I lived my life without regard to how I would end up eternally. I think back on my life before I really got serious about my salvation, and it scares me to know I lived for the moment. Some of my actions could have easily taken me out of here. I know now that God kept me here for a reason, but at the time, it was hard for me to think beyond the moment. I had self-esteem issues and very little confidence in my early life. I learned rather quickly that some of the people I hung out with did not have my best interest at heart. I also learned that money, possessions and notoriety are really not as important as I once thought they were.

Over the years, I have been through so many situations, but without God as my deliverer, stronghold and rock, I would not be here today. He was there even when I did not realize it. Psalm 46:1 (KJV) says, *"God is our refuge and strength, A very present help in trouble."* I now rely on the word of God as I take this journey in this thing called life. The Psalms have been my source of strength many days.

As you will see, my journey has not always been on a straight path. There were a lot of twists and turns around corners and one-way streets. Those who know me may look at my life today and think I have it altogether. They may think I have been where I am all the time, but that is not so. Also, there are those who think they know me and where I came from, but they are also quite mistaken. You do not know my story or my struggles. You do not know how the LORD has brought me from my insecurities, my self-esteem issues, hurts, and shortcomings to becoming confident in Him. This book is not to address them but to encourage those who are going through their own personal struggles.

I do understand it is hard to encourage others without being a little bit transparent, and I know transparency can be scary because you never know how people will use your words, your life, your failures, or your shortcomings against you or for their own benefit. That is why I encouraged myself to stand and say whatever, boldly moving forward without hesitation or concern. I pray that whatever the LORD puts on my heart and in my hand will be a blessing to those who read this book. I learned that our story is best told in segments.

"I heard an unknown voice say, Now I will take the load from your shoulders; I will free your hands from their heavy tasks. You cried to me in trouble, and I saved you." - Psalm 81:5b-7a (NLT)

When I was a few months old, I had some medical issues. I had surgery at a young age and was hospitalized for several days. I do not know the whole story, but I know I am still here. I still have medical issues, but I have been able to carry out all that God has given me to do. Apparently, from the beginning, God had a plan for my life. Little did I know or understand that everything I was going to experience would mold me into who I am today. I now count all that I have been through as lessons learned. But I have to say, all I have been through have prepared me for such a time as this. This book speaks to the heart of my salvation.

This is to encourage you to trust in the LORD with all your heart and soul and to keep walking with your head up confidently, even when you do not feel like it. This book of encouragement is not in any special order. It is just like life. You see, the moments when you need to be encouraged the most do not just happen in any special order.

I want to encourage others as I encourage myself to grow in God's grace and accept His forgiveness and mercy that He so freely gives, which sometimes feels so hard to accept. I do not always feel like I am worthy of all that God is blessing me with, but I know feelings are not what I am supposed to be depending on when it comes to His love for me.

"The Lord appeared to us in the past, saying:
'I have loved you with an everlasting love; I have drawn
you with unfailing kindness.'" Jeremiah 31:3

CHAPTER 1
FINDING THE TRUTH

I learned at an early age that it is important to study for yourself.

Isaiah 55:8-9 "For my thoughts are not your thoughts, neither are your ways my ways," declares the Lord. "As the heavens are higher than the earth, so are my ways higher than your ways and my thoughts than your thoughts."

Thinking about life looking backwards, I see how God has always been there walking beside me and even carrying me at times. I am not perfect, never said I was, never pretended I was, and surely never acted like I was. But, I am perfectly made in God's image. I grew up in a small town, and everybody knew everybody back then. I grew up in church. My parents made sure of that. You see, my mom is Methodist and my dad is Baptist. Because I grew up in a small town, the churches fellowshipped together from time to time. I attended both churches as a young girl, but mainly my mom's church.

As I think back, there was so much I did not understand about the word of God. I knew what was told to me, and I am not so sure it was really the truth. The explanations I received when I asked questions were pretty interesting! And yes, I asked a lot of questions. I believed in heaven and hell. Back then, I kind of thought most of us young people were on our way to hell, as some adults would say. Not that we were any worse than the adults who judged us, but at the time, we did not know their stories, and we were taught to respect our elders. One thing I do know is we all have a story and a recording that we do not want God to playback.

Once I started reading and studying for myself, there was one thing I understood - none of us have the right to judge others regardless of who you are. I remember reading in the Bible for the first time *Romans 3:10 which says, "As it is written, there is none righteous, no, not one."* And *verse 23, "For all have sinned, and come short of the glory of God."* I had wondered why we pretend we or certain people are so perfect. That is what I did not and still do not understand. What I learned is once you truly begin to trust God and follow Jesus, facades will fall, and secret sins will be revealed. It is important to treat people with respect and not think more highly of ourselves than we ought to think. Because bottom line, we are all sinners saved by grace. It does not matter how much money you have, how much land you possess, nor how many titles you have. One thing is for sure, all those things mean nothing in the sight of the LORD, and they will not get you into heaven or give you eternal life. Although I have been through a lot of different things in and out of the church, let's be honest. Many of us can say that some of the most difficult times we had as we tried to get ourselves together came from those whom we trusted inside of the church building. This was just the beginning. I specified church building because the people inside are the church, the 'bride of Christ'.

I learned that the Bride of Christ is a metaphor that illustrates the relationship between Jesus and His followers, the Church. Jesus, the bridegroom, loves His bride by offering Himself as a sacrifice for her (Ephesians 5:25–27).

Unfortunately, we often get confused and leave the church building because of the people of 'the church' who, by the way, are a group of imperfect followers of Jesus just like us. 1 Peter 1:24-25 (NIV) says, *"For all people are like grass, and all their glory is like the flowers of the field; the grass withers and the flowers fall, but the word of the Lord endures forever."* I have read and heard people say if you leave, you were worshipping people, not God. Well, that is not necessarily true. It all depends on the situation in which you leave. Sometimes, it is a personal attack by one or two. Sometimes, it is not personal but something someone experiences. Sometimes, it is just hard to worship where there is confusion, discord, and mean-spirited people. Sometimes, those who are supposed to be leading are not acting very godly toward people by how they treat others, how they talk to others, or how they talk about others. All of this gives those who are trying to get their life together a false sense of what the church is about. And yes, sometimes people use that as an excuse to leave the church, but in that case, it is on them and not those who are trying to help them come closer to a loving Savior.

The Bible tells us God is loving, merciful, and not a respecter of persons, but if you are new in the church, some individuals can make it hard for others to understand this. That is why it is important how those who have been in the church and who are true followers of Jesus, treat each other because new converts are watching. This also affects relationships with other Christians because I know for me, although I may have stayed, it took a while to trust others because of some. And unfortunately, sometimes you do not want to talk to anybody connected to any church. There is a healing process in either case; a time to step back and reflect on the One who really matters, the One who heals, the One who saves, and the One who makes you whole – Jesus.

2 Timothy 3:14-15 (NIV) says, *"But as for you, continue in what you have learned and have become convinced of, because you know those from whom you learned it, and how from infancy you have known the Holy Scriptures, which are able to make you wise for salvation through faith in Christ Jesus."* Some people may not feel the pain should be real, but it is real to that person, trust me.

Think about it. Who do you go to when you are hurt inside the church? How do you heal from such pain?

What if the pain does not seem to go away? How do you help someone else who is going through this?

CHAPTER 2
MY CROOKED PATH

Our path is not always a straight line.

Psalm 77:11-12 says, "I will remember the deeds of the Lord; yes, I will remember your miracles of long ago. I will consider all your works and meditate on all your mighty deeds."

Some of us grew up with a lot of issues in our childhood: losses, disappointments, prejudices, family secrets, family drama, town secrets, and so on. Some people can handle all of this and move on without a second thought, some need constant words of encouragement, and others need professional help. I have been through all the emotions, and some things were easier to handle than others. But one thing is for sure, we all need God. He has brought us through despite some of our own failures, trials and errors of life. I am sure thankful for that!

I remember being quiet about situations I was going through. I was depressed and not able to talk about what I had been through because I knew if I spoke about it, I would become vulnerable. People often use other people's weaknesses against them, and I did not want that to happen to me. People assume things anyway, especially when they do not know the true story, and sometimes we just allow them to live in their own lies about us. People whisper as they are counting us out but pretending in public to be for us. As for me, they miscalculated as they counted me out, because my God had other plans. *Jeremiah 29:11-13 says; "For I know the plans I have for you, declares the Lord, plans to prosper you and not to harm you, plans to give you hope and a future. Then you will call on me and come and pray to me, and I will listen to you. You will seek me and find me when you seek me with all your heart."*

I finished high school with an A average and even received a scholarship for college. I wanted to go away to school, but because I did not want to be too far away from my child - whom I birthed at an early age - I went to school close by. I am thankful I was able to go to college. My child was a blessing in my life, and I know that because of my love and commitment to him and his sister. I knew I had to do all that I could to make sure they had everything they needed in life and not ever want for anything. There were some difficult days and long nights, but I know things could have been worse if I did not have my parents and our village to support us. Always remember, *you "can do all things through Christ who strengthens you".* I learned to not allow what others say or do affect what I do for my family or myself.

I did not realize until later in years that God still loved me throughout my life and was carrying me through despite all the detours I took, the fake friends I encountered, the many disappointments, and the mistakes I made. I know God did not create some of the situations, but He allowed them to be so and used them for His glory in my life. How great it would have been if I could have avoided most of what I have been through. But then again, to avoid any part of what I have been through, I would have missed the good days, the good times, the special people who were a part of my journey, and all these lessons I needed to learn.

I had self-esteem issues at one time. I did not believe in myself even with all that I had already come through and accomplished. Although I did well in school, started working part time at 15 years old at a company I eventually retired from, had both parents who owned their home, and had a few friends, I still had some underlying issues. I looked at myself as an ugly duckling, and there were so many things I hid from my family and my friends. I compared myself to others who seemed to be popular and more confident. People did not seem to pay much attention or ask about your mental health or well-being back then. I was afraid to ask for help because I did not want anyone to know what was going on. I did not want people to look at me differently. You see, I just hid my feelings well. But one thing I did learn was I had so much to be thankful for.

CHAPTER 3
GOD, HELP ME

Please, LORD, straighten my life out.

Over the years, I took the negative things I heard others say about me and some of the things I saw to heart. Alone, I could not fight the bad things in my life or in my mind. I remember crying out to God with tears flowing, losing all control, falling into a fetal position, and not knowing if He heard me or even cared. Those moments when I felt like everything was on my shoulders, I wondered how I could make it. Will things ever get better? Should I even wait to see?

I felt like David as he cried out in Psalm 6:6-7 (NIV), *"I am worn out from my groaning. All night long I flood my bed with weeping and drench my couch with tears. My eyes grow weak with sorrow; they fail because of all my foes."* And although David spoke of his physical enemies, I was dealing with all the issues going on in my mind.

Prayer became important to me, but it was an uphill battle. I was not always sure what or how to pray so I leaned on the Psalms, ones like Psalm 42: 1-4a (NIV), *"As the deer pants for streams of water, so my soul pants for you, my God. My soul thirsts for God, for the living God. When can I go and meet with God? My tears have been my food day and night, while people say to me all day long, 'Where is your God?' These things I remember as I pour out my soul."* I just learned to cry out to God, especially in those moments when I needed Him most.

When we do not feel our best, we do things to make us feel better, or so we think. I was not happy about how I looked at one time. I was always trying to improve myself because I did not think I was pretty enough or good enough. I had to learn that God created me the way I am - my looks and appearance - and I needed to realize I was wonderfully made, created in His image. I am a designer original! *Psalm 139:13-16 (NIV)* says, *"For you created my inmost being; you knit me together in my mother's womb. I praise you because I am fearfully and wonderfully made; your works are wonderful, I know that full well. My frame was not hidden from you when I was made in the secret place, when I was woven together in the depths of the earth. Your eyes saw my unformed body; all the days ordained for me were written in your book before one of them came to be."*

I had to read that Scripture over and over and truly believe it. I had to take the word of the LORD and not man. Years ago, all the magazines, television commercials, and shows would suggest how we should look, how we should dress, what we should consume, and even what we should bathe in. Now Facebook, TikTok, and other social media platforms have since added to this narrative. And, if you did not look like everybody else, there must have been something wrong with you. When you are young, you start making decisions for yourself. Most of the time you think you know it all, but believe me, you do not! You will fall into that same downward spiral. I had to learn that the only person that I will have a relationship with my whole life and the only one that matters Is me! I had to know, understand and accept myself; the person God created me to be and the one He created in His image. And I learned not to define myself by any one moment in time.

For me, thankfully, I did have the foundation of the church. Along with a little bit of faith, I had some of the tools, although I was not quite sure how to use them. But, apparently God was protecting me for such a time as this. He provided me with a couple of spiritual moms who prayed with and for me and who guided me into the next phase of my journey. I was able to talk freely about things I had not ever shared with anyone. That freed me to begin the steps to forgiveness - not only others but myself.

Today, there are so many avenues for help and guidance. There are spiritual counselors, youth support groups, churches, and associations that offer all kinds of help for young people who are going through all sorts of issues and need to talk before they get to the point of no return. You can learn how to deal with stress and pressure, incorporate self-care, focus on your mental health, build healthy relationships, and overcome challenges and difficulties. I did not have those opportunities back then. I thought my life was over at times, and I was all over the place.

As I encountered a few twists and turns during my journey (that is putting it mildly), there were times I did not think I would make it physically nor mentally. I was on my own, trying to find my way, and getting caught up in things I did not quite understand. Situations that could have ruined me for life. I know

now I was allowing the world to pull me into a place of no return. What I did not know was that God still had His hands on me.

The hardest and most hurtful experience was when people - those I thought were closest to me - were talking with the crowd rather than them helping me. *"Yes, I knew that's how she was!" "It's a shame!" "I could have told you that!"* I had to believe Psalm 46. Verse 1 says, *"God is our refuge and strength, an ever-present help in trouble."* The writer tells us throughout this Psalm that God *is* our strength, not only just *gives* us strength. He is unchanging regardless of what is going on around us. Even though we are continually afflicted or struggling, God is there strengthening us. He is faithful. He loves us despite our seasons of stillness, and He helps us to persevere through them.

I thank God for bringing to my remembrance that as long as I have breath, there is hope. Never allow one incident, one mistake, one person, nor one thing determine your destiny. As I learned to focus on God and His word, my faith got a little bit stronger.

CHAPTER 4
ANSWERED PRAYER

I have to thank God for the positive people during
those times when I needed them.

After a while, the life I was living stopped being
fulfilling. I started to realize that if I was not going
along with the crowd, the crowd was not going
along with me. The more I went after things, the
harder it became. I knew there was something
more, but frankly, I did not know what it was. A good
friend of mine who I grew up with since
kindergarten (she has since gone home to be with
the LORD), contacted me. We had a few issues at
one time that we had to work through, like most
teens go through with their friends. If you are really
true friends, you work through your issues. Upset
with each other one moment, going out to dinner
the next. We reconnected, talked through our
issues, prayed together, and started attending
several different churches out of the area. We were
both searching for purpose and direction in our

lives. I thank God for her and the times we spent together as this was the beginning of my spiritual journey of searching for real truth and eternal life. One night while we were at this one particular church during a service of healing, I prayed for the LORD to forgive me for my sins and all the wrong I had done, to heal me, and to accept me as His child. I found myself in tears and speaking in tongues, finally realizing how much He loved me. People were praying for me, and I do not exactly remember much after that. All I know is He forgave me, lifted a burden off me, and changed my life forever.

I learned way back then that God puts certain people in your life at different times to fulfill specific assignments. Well, at that moment, I did not realize nor understand it. It was only later that I fully appreciated those moments in time. She was a good friend. God put her in my life to make sure I would stay connected to Him by leading me to other positive people without even realizing the impact at that time she had on my life. I look back at all the things she accomplished for God, and I am thankful and grateful that she was so instrumental in my journey.

As we visited different churches, I met other people who became part of my journey, and I thank God for each one of them and their roles in my growth. I met a lady at one of the churches who guided me further into studying. She led me to attend a Bible college where I received my bachelor's degree in Theology. Since then, I have furthered my Christian education at Liberty University. She became one of my true close friends, confidantes, and encouragers to this day.

"Ointment and perfume rejoice the heart: so doth the sweetness of a man's friend by hearty counsel."
- Proverbs 27:9 (KJV)

Dear Heavenly Father, I thank you for those you put in my life as guiding lights. I do not take them, nor the lessons taught/learned for granted. There are women that have been instrumental in my walk with you, and some have since went home to glory, and I am thankful that they knew how special they were and their part in my journey. In Jesus' name, I pray. Amen.

Sometimes, we are close to people growing up but they may not be the ones walking with us once we have matured. It does not mean they are not still our friends. It only means their path is different, and we cannot take offense when they do things without us that we used to share in. That is when we realize we have changed. God has rearranged our thinking, our life, and our path, and it is evident to others that we are not the same people we were. That is actually a good thing! We should be thankful for our transformation. Although God created us all, people can see the Christ in us and respect where God has taken us. A change has come over me! Thank you Lord!

There are still some folks who live in the past, and because they refuse to get their life together, they will try to bring you back also. They will try to tell your story, and although they cannot tell it better than you, they will try! Do not be surprised when you find out not everybody will be shouting with joy and celebrating with you. Continue to go forward as Paul stated in Philippians 3:12-14 (KJV), *"Not as though I had already attained, either were already perfect: but I follow after, if that I may apprehend that for which also I am apprehended of Christ Jesus. Brethren, I count not myself to have apprehended: but this one thing I do, forgetting those things which are behind, and reaching forth unto those things which are before, I press toward the mark for the prize of the high calling of God in Christ Jesus."*

LORD God, I have been through so many things in my life, and I did not think I could make it through some of the rough days. As I look back, I realize you brought me through every one of them. How can I not trust you? How can I not have faith in a God who has proven His love for me by sending His Son to die for my sins? I love you, LORD, I give you all honor, glory and praise. In Jesus' name, I pray. Amen.

My salvation and my honor depend on God; he is my mighty rock, my refuge. Psalm 62:7 (NIV)

As my life journey continued, I admit, I made some more mistakes. All of us have experienced going left when we knew what was right. I had some good times. When you are younger, you just want to be a part of the crowd, but you learn fast if you are paying attention that the crowd is always going in the wrong direction. Not only is it the wrong direction but it is a strange and dangerous path, but I have to say, I am thankful for all of it. Not that I am glad I went through some bad times but without them, I could not appreciate where I am now.

Now that I am older, I am thankful for the people God has put in my life to support me through this next phase of life. Of course, there are some who have been there all the time. But, there is a special group of ladies in my life, and if I had not met and spent time with them, I know I would not have written this book.

It is refreshing to spend time with women who have each other's best interest at heart. We encourage each other. We push one another to ensure we are working toward our goals. Even though we are all writers, we have different goals. It does not matter what each person is doing. We genuinely support and pray for one another. We may not always be in the same room, but there is always a sense of closeness. One of the women in our group shared a great African proverb once. It really spoke to us. The African proverb stated, *"If you want to go fast, go alone; if you want to go far, go together."* We want to go far, therefore, we are willing to go together. When we talk about our writing, we share information to figure out the best direction. I learned that my voice and story matter. My words must live beyond these pages.

The world needs more women that are willing to support, uplift and encourage each other. Women should be excited to see other women turn a page in their chapter or fulfill their dreams.

There was another woman who was there for me when I needed support. She came to my house periodically to check on my progress. She checked my writing for mistakes and made sure I met my deadlines. I am thankful and grateful for these women who not only wanted to see me win, but did what they could to make it happen. I learned that my vision had to be followed by action. It was not enough for me to stand at the bottom of the stairway and look up. I actually had to climb the stairs to get to the top. I quickly learned that there were individuals in the world willing to help me climb the stairway.

CHAPTER 5
PATH TO FORGIVENESS

I learned how my faith led to forgiveness.

Forgiveness is the act of excusing or pardoning others in spite of their shortcomings. From a theological perspective, forgiveness refers to God's pardon of the sins of mankind.

Many people have mistreated me in the past. There were also times when I made mistakes. In some situations, things that happened were not my fault. I know it was not what God planned for me. He took the bad and worked it out for my good. When things happen, we cannot let it impact our purpose in life. We should only allow God to lead and guide us. When people say negative things about you, be encouraged. You are inferior to no one. You do measure up because God has raised you up. It is okay to admit if you did not always feel this way. There are some people in the world who are cruel and do not care about others. They uttered whispers they thought you did not hear. When people you thought were on your side, the ones you thought you could talk to, share with, and feel comfortable around were talking about you behind your back to others who you knew you could not trust. If this is you, let me encourage you with this simple prayer below:

Dear God, there are some people that I find it a bit difficult to forgive. Please purify my heart and soul of resentment, bitterness and anger. Please help me release the pain of past hurt so I can forgive and move on. I thank you, God, for forgiving me as I learn to forgive. In Jesus' name, I pray. Amen.

Now that I am older, it is easier for me to speak to people who I know talked about me. In my youth, these things impacted my mind and self-esteem. That is another story for a different book. I thank God for caring about my concerns and comforting me when I was wounded by the ignorance of people. And although I have moved on and have grown closer to God, I can see those same people, smile, and have peace. We all have to decide what is best for us in moments like this. It was best for me to put my trust in God, not man.

I use to wonder how I would forgive the people who did bad things to me. Was I supposed to forgive people who acted like they did nothing wrong? How could I forgive myself for allowing people to treat me this way? This was difficult. I was trapped in a prison without bars. At one point, I convinced myself I was not going to forgive anyone. I was in a space where I did not care what happened to them. Although I read Scriptures such as Ephesians 4:32, *"And be ye kind one to another, tenderhearted, forgiving one another, even as God for Christ's sake hath forgiven you,"* it was still very hard to forgive.

Another Scripture that came to mind was Matthew 18: 21-22, *"Then Peter came to Jesus and asked, 'Lord, how many times shall I forgive my brother or sister who sins against me? Up to seven times?' Jesus answered, 'I tell you, not seven times, but seventy-seven times.'"* In addition, there were other Scriptures, such as Romans 12:14 (KJV) which states, *"Bless them which persecute you: bless, and curse not."*

Even though people have persecuted me, Romans 12:17 tells us not to repay evil with evil. However, I kept trying to figure out what to do to get back at those who hurt me. Since I am human, it was natural for me to want to seek revenge. I was not ready to forgive. I learned quickly that unforgiveness not only affected me, it affected other relationships as well. I found myself treating people unfairly based on my experiences with those who mistreated me. Then, I read a Scripture that reminded me what I had to lose. 1 Peter 3:9 (HCSB) states, *"Not paying back evil for evil or insult for insult but, on the contrary, giving a blessing, since you were called for this, so that you can inherit a blessing."* Finally, I realized unforgiveness was all futile and a total waste of time and energy. Besides, no one cared.

I was saved, believed in Jesus, went to church, studied the Bible, but I still dealt with faith issues. Some of these issues came from individuals in the church. I learned that I was looking in the wrong direction. I had put too much faith in man rather than in God. I looked to man for acceptance and confirmation when I should have been looking to God. Individuals in the church were just like me. We were all human, which meant we all had flaws. I learned that I had to look to Jesus and have faith only in Him.

It was important for me to only depend on the Holy Spirit and His guidance. Romans 1:17 reminds us that we need to learn how to live from faith to faith. Everything we do should be approached with faith. This includes forgiving. I learned to trust God's word on a different level. Changing my focus made a big difference in my life. It took me a while to get to a point where I was no longer trapped in unforgiveness. I call it a trap because as long as I did not forgive people, they controlled me. When I allowed others to control my emotions, I started acting outside of my true character. While I allowed anger to eat me up inside, others were living their lives without a thought of how they treated me. It was imperative for me to disconnect from all negative relationships; to no longer remain negatively connected with anyone. It was like drinking poison and expecting the other person to die, but they did not. Instead, I got sicker. It was like a cyst in the pit of my stomach that continued to grow. It got bigger because I was not getting the antidote (the word). It started affecting other parts of my body as it grew. It started clogging up my veins and cutting off the blood flow until my strength was depleted. I had to do better. Forgiving is a hard process to master without the help of the Holy Spirit.

How could I call myself a Christian woman who ministered to others, but held grudges? How did I expect God to forgive me if I refused to forgive His children? This was a critical element for me to learn. To properly heal and move forward in a positive way, it was necessary for me to put my complete trust in Jesus. I had faith that He would give me peace in the midst of it all. I knew this would not be an overnight transition. It would take some time. It was vital for me to finally be free. I had to bestow God's mercy and grace upon those who hurt me and pray for them.

Jesus admonishes us to forgive those we have issues with so He can forgive our transgressions. In Mark 11:25 (KJV), He said, *"And when ye stand praying, forgive, if ye have ought against any: that your Father also which is in heaven may forgive you your trespasses."* I had to pray for strength that only comes from the Father through the Holy Spirit. I also had to accept God's forgiveness for myself which was the hardest part.

Even though I was willing to forgive others, there was still a part of me that felt I was unworthy of the same forgiveness. It took quite some time for me to learn. I learned that nothing is beyond God's forgiveness. I had to allow myself to forgive my past mistakes and behaviors. I was not proud of my actions, but I learned to give myself grace. Charles Stanley wrote, and I had to accept, *"No sin is too great, too awful, or too prolific for God to forgive. No person is so deep in sin, so ingrained in a lifestyle, so steeped in evil, that he or she cannot be saved."* Is there someone you need to forgive? Is there something you need to forgive yourself for? Just remember, forgiveness is not a feeling. It is a decision. Whatever grudge, bitterness, or resentment you have toward someone will not go away without a choice to let it go. Choose today: freedom or bondage.

Take a moment and pray to be released from the bondage of unforgiveness.

Dear Heavenly Father, I pray for those who have done me wrong In the past and, I pray only the best for them. I forgive them, and I am letting go of the anger and any hatred that I felt against them. I know that if I expect you to forgive me when I am not deserving, I have to be willing to forgive those who have done me wrong. I understand that if I want to continue to be used by you, I have to emulate Jesus who was an example of true forgiveness when He died for my sins. In whose name I pray. Amen.

A Lot of Other Spirits Out There

I was asked to speak to a group of women during a time when I was trying to get myself together. I did not know what I was going to say, but I prayed and asked God for direction and guidance.

I prayed, read, studied and prayed some more, but nothing happened. I could not focus. I could not write. I took a moment to just be still and listen. God said to me, *"My daughter, this is personal."* I said to Him, *"Father, it is difficult for me to share my shortcomings and deal with deceptive spirits in others."* He said to me, *"Why is it hard for you to share your shortcomings?"* In that moment, I was reminded that we all have sinned and come short of the glory of God.

As I stood looking in the mirror while I combed my hair, I thought about my mission. It was crucial for me to be open and honest with the women I would be speaking to. It was essential that they were aware of the tricks and confusion from the enemy and how to be victorious in spite of it. I reflected on my past. Often times, I felt defeated due to money challenges, the energy I spent with my therapist, and needing to take prescribed medication. But, I knew I needed to practice more positive thinking.

We live in a fallen, imperfect, and cursed world. There is death, corruption, demonic spirits, and evil. It is unfortunate that people live life on the dark side. However, we all have a choice. Most of us were not taught about spirits growing up in our churches. The truth was we did not want to hear about these things. One of the first things I learned about in church was the Holy Spirit. It was necessary to get acclimated with who He was first.

I learned that one of the greatest assurances of the eternal security of the believer is the fact that the Father has sealed every believer with the Holy Spirit. People should be able to tell that there is something different about us, a change that comes from the inside. The whole concept of sealing includes the ideas of ownership, authority and security, and since God has sealed us, we belong to Him. People often quote Scriptures concerning the Holy Spirit, but do not truly have the spirit on the inside.

We all go through things we do not understand. There are times when things are turned upside down, and I feel like I am going to lose my mind. I know this is spiritual warfare. People attend retreats year after year, attempting to gain a renewal. During the retreat, individuals were on fire for the LORD and felt empowered. Sadly, when the retreat was over, the fire was diminished. It was a temporary renewal. After attending retreats year after year and not being fulfilled spiritually, I knew it was time to seek the Holy Spirit for myself. I learned that the Holy Spirit was a representation of God. The third person in the trinity. He is also eternal. He is omnipotent, omniscient and omnipresent (all powerful, all knowing, and everywhere). Jesus promised us in John 14:26, *"But the Helper, the Holy Spirit, whom the Father will send in My name, He will teach you all things and bring to your remembrance all things that I said to you."* I knew I needed something more in my life.

I needed the empowerment that only came from the Holy Spirit and ultimately from the blood of Jesus. Acts 1:8 says, **"But you shall receive power when the Holy Spirit has come upon you; and you shall be witnesses to Me in Jerusalem, and in all Judea and Samaria, and to the end of the earth."** The power of the Holy Spirit was given to enable us to be effective witnesses for Jesus Christ. He gave us the power to overcome mental illness, jealousy, envy, strife, misery, defiance, bitterness, bondage, lying and pride. These are all spirits that we fail to recognize. We are used to the world talking about feelings or emotions. We were never really taught these things were tactics from the devil to immobilize us. It is a roadblock to prevent us from carrying out our mission for God.

The Holy Spirit will also make you an effective witness for Christ. He will give us power as long as we are willing to be used as a witness and bear fruit.

There are spirits we encounter every day. Often, we are unaware of the tricks and tools the devil uses to interrupt our joy and peace throughout the day. For example, we may leave home happy and in a great mood, but encounter someone during the day who leaves us feeling emotionally, physically and spiritually drained. This is a trick of the devil. Another trick of the devil is when people hurt us but refuse to take accountability for their actions. In these situations, an apology goes a long way. However, there are so many people who do not know how to apologize when they have done wrong.

Have you encountered rejection or jealousy from a sister or brother and did not know why? Have you ever received a message from someone who left you feeling apprehensive? Have you ever felt used by someone physically or emotionally? Have you ever met a person who tried to convince you of their superior spiritual status and why you should follow him or her instead of God? Have you ever encountered someone looking for weaknesses to determine if you were unhappy? These are not coincidences. These are spirits. I spoke on spirits a few years ago. My research was quite interesting. I was warned not to get too deep into the background of spirits. It was enlightening to learn that some spirits have names, while others do not.

I quickly learned it is necessary to be filled with the Holy Spirit to combat these other spirits. The Holy Spirit has equipped individuals with the power to fight spirits sent by the devil. He has to have complete rule over your thoughts and your life to empower you.

From the perspective of daily living and a vital Christian experience, the filling of the Holy Spirit is a vital component. This is the essence of true spirituality and the basic requirement for growth and maturity.

Lord, thank You for showing me what Satan is looking for, those of us who are alone and those who are lost. We do not always realize how vulnerable we are when we are alone. Thanks for showing us that we need each other. Please help me to help others realize this important reality: there is a danger in trying to be a Christian all alone. In Jesus' name. Amen.

"Not forsaking the assembling of ourselves together, as the manner of some is; but exhorting one another: and so much the more, as ye see the day approaching." Hebrews 10:25 (KJV)

CHAPTER 6
BEING FREE

There is nothing like being free.

We often question what we have done wrong when we go through painful situations. There are times when we know we have done nothing wrong. Yet, we still go through things, nonetheless. It is common to fight back or give up, especially when people are mistreating us. However, God says, *"Be still."* He then calls us to draw close and absorb the truths within the Scriptures. When we do that, it allows us to believe in God's power. *"Yours, Lord, is the greatness and the power and the glory and the majesty and the splendor, for everything in heaven and earth is yours. Yours, LORD, is the kingdom; you are exalted as head over all."* 1 Chronicles 29:11 (NIV)

The truth about us is revealed in a crisis. When I paid close attention during turmoil, I learned valuable lessons about how to deal with conflicts within myself and others in the future.

I went through something major that could have damaged my reputation. I immediately wanted to defend myself. It was necessary for me to let everyone know I was not the person being portrayed by others. I was in a space of trying to prove myself to man, but I knew my position with God. I knew my view of God was not distorted. God only allows people to go so far when they are attempting to destroy His children. Even though I knew God would protect me, I was still ready to quit. God said to me, *"Be still. This is not your destination but a part of your journey. Hold your peace for the battle is not yours but the Lords."* God reassured me that I did not have to defend myself. He encouraged me to talk to Him and meditate on His word.

As I was enduring all I was going through, I heard, "Trust your struggle." So, I continued to trust in the LORD, holding on to see where He was leading me.

I often meditate on Psalm 62:5-8 (NKJV). Then I wait for God to speak to my heart and give me His peace. *"My soul, wait silently for God alone. For my expectation is from Him. He only is my rock and my salvation; He is my defense; I shall not be moved. In God is my salvation and my glory. The rock of my strength, and my refuge, is in God. Trust in Him at all times, you people; Pour out your heart before Him; God is a refuge for us."*

There was a time when I struggled to trust Christian leaders. Their words did not match their behaviors. It was so easy for them to change. It was hard to believe in people who had no credibility. It was challenging dealing with people with jealous traits. But God! He showed me that even if people did not support me, they could not block the things He had for me. When God removed negative people from my life, He replaced them with someone better.

God knew I needed to endure the challenges to strengthen me. The challenges helped develop my endurance and built my confidence. The people who treated me badly assisted me in becoming more like Jesus. I was so grateful for the lessons I learned. It was such a humbling experience. God uses challenges to help us grow. It is necessary that we be careful when calling individuals our friends. This was such a tough lesson for me to learn. God's presence gave me so much peace. It was refreshing and encouraging. I learned it was critical for me to be still. He knows what is best for us at all times. His presence enables us to show love in the face of abuse, have patience in the midst of stress, and execute positive change. Experiencing the presence of God helped me handle things the way He wanted me to handle them. I allowed the Holy Spirit to lead me. I felt good knowing that God used me.

People are comfortable using and abusing others. It is so easy for them to move on to the next victim. I realized I cared too much about relationships that held no substance. This taught me to back off people, especially individuals in the church. I had to continually remind myself I was somebody important. Most importantly, I am a child of the Most High King. I now refuse to allow anyone to make me feel less than His child.

Dear heavenly Father, you created me uniquely and you fashioned me in my mother's womb. I thank you for creating me in your image, and I know I am someone special. I cannot allow anyone to make me question my worth. I know I am special in your eyes and that is all that matters. Amen.

"He restoreth my soul: he leadeth me in the paths of righteousness for his name's sake." Psalm 23:3

Have you ever felt forgotten about or left out? I can truly relate. I thought I was closer to certain people until they showed me differently. Initially, I was hurt. Sometimes we hurt our own feelings thinking we mean more to people than we really do! There were women in my circle who purposely excluded me from outings. When I was invited to certain events, I was left out of group conversations. It seemed that even though the invitation was extended to me, they were hoping I did not attend. Their intentions were not pure. I could not understand why I was excluded. Then, I realized I had to let it go and put my trust in God. I knew He would never let me down.

God put people in our lives who genuinely care. Those who are meant to travel through life with us will be there to do so. God will remove Individuals who are not meant to be a part of the journey. We must lean on God and understand He is in control. Often, we try to hold on to people when God wants us to let them go. Some people are only meant to be in our lives for a season, to be a blessing, or teach us a lesson. We must figure this out sooner than later. This is a painful process to go through, but I am encouraged.

I remind myself of God's word. Ephesians 2:19-20 (NIV) states, *"Consequently, you are no longer foreigners and strangers, but fellow citizens with God's people and also members of his household, built on the foundation of the apostles and prophets, with Christ Jesus himself as the chief cornerstone."*

Once I realized who I was in Christ, I stopped looking for acceptance from other sources. I was no longer concerned with being a part of groups. I was done seeking validation from others. I learned to follow my own path. I was finally content with the person God created me to be. I was grateful and thankful to God for His peace that surpasses all understanding. He opened the doors I thought were closed. He connected me with positive, genuine, and like-minded individuals. Like Psalm 118:8 states, *"It is better to trust in the Lord than to put confidence in man."*

There was a time in my life when I was very angry with myself. I made many mistakes and wrong choices. I put my trust in people, and as a result, I got hurt. I was angry with myself because I did not protect myself. I did not recognize my worth. Now that I realize whose I am, I stand firm on my worth. I am no longer hurt when people exclude me. I learned to only trust in God, Jesus, and the Holy Spirit. I also learned that healing comes from the lessons we learn along the way.

It is not necessary to discuss all the things that I have been through. It is important to share the details of how I transformed. Transformation means to change. We must make changes to ensure our character and behaviors are pleasing to God. When we transform, it is inward change that manifests itself on the outside. The Holy Spirit who dwells within us is who we depend on to guide us through this process. I must admit, there were times when I felt like I was going backward. However, those instances were necessary for my personal growth. When I felt like things were not moving fast enough, I learned not to get discouraged. I stayed in the word and trusted the process. I am intentional when I do things. I am mindful of how I speak.

Romans 12:2 tells us not to be conformed to this world, but to be transformed by the renewing of our mind. If I allow the Holy Spirit to use me, I will be transformed. When we conform to the world, it is not who we are, but what we are doing. 2 Corinthians 3:17 (KJV) says, *"Now the Lord is that Spirit: and where the Spirit of the Lord is, there is liberty."* Liberty means to be set free from ugly attitudes, personalities, actions and reactions. He will always set us free.

Marvin Winans, "Just Don't Wanna Know" is a song that resonates with me a lot when I am dealing with things.   One of the verses states, *"You ignored all my tears, hoping they would disappear. I guess you just didn't want to know. I learned I could cope and discovered I could make it. It was cold and lonely, but I wouldn't change a thing, not for the knowledge that I learned. I learned I could grow. I can't say how, but I'm over it now."* One morning I woke up and I felt free.

CHAPTER 7
LESSONS LEARNED

I'm thankful for the lessons learned along the way.

I have walked through the waters of insecurity, low self-esteem, and other negative feelings. I am so grateful I am no longer that person. I am enough, and God sees me even when people do not. My voice matters, and my story is making a difference. I learned that although our journeys may be different, our destination is the same. We should encourage each other along the way. God teaches us lessons daily if we just pay attention. It is important to just be still and watch things unfold. That is when we realize some things are not what they seem. I learned that I needed to celebrate myself and my accomplishments even when others did not. I learned to believe in myself. I will never forget my worth again. I started to set boundaries. I learned to stop putting people in places in my life where they should not be. It was necessary to read the writing on the wall.

I learned from my parents to be kind, courteous, compassionate, loving and giving. When I was growing up, there were years when our home was open to young people who needed temporary housing. My parents received calls day and night and worked hard to accommodate the situation. I must admit, it was a hard adjustment. There were several shifts in our household to take care of others. I learned at an early age just how compassionate my parents were. We did not have a lot, but they were eager to share with others. Our home was always the place where our friends and family from near and far gathered. From coffee in the morning to dinner in the evening, our home was the ideal place for get-togethers.

My mom had many sayings when we were coming up. My siblings and I had such a great time laughing and listening to the things she used to say. *"Make sure you treat people right. You never know who you will need before you leave this world."* As I think back on this, the parable of the rich man and Lazarus in Luke 16:19-31 comes to mind. In this story, a rich man lived in a mansion, while a poor beggar laid at his gate desiring to be fed the scraps from the rich man's table. The beggar was overlooked, but he put his trust in God. He knew someday he would be delivered. Eventually, they both died. The beggar went to heaven and the rich man ended up in hell. The rich man asked Abraham to have Lazarus give him water and send him to warn his brothers, so they would not come to the same place of torment. He believed if they heard from a dead man, they would repent. The moral of the story was a person could possess all the riches in the world, but if a person rejects God, they will not see the kingdom of heaven. God has preachers, teachers and missionaries here on earth to carry out His word of salvation. It is up to each of us to accept Jesus while there is still time here on earth.

My mom always went to church and made sure we were there, too. She sang in the choir, was a stewardess, cooked in the kitchen, attended Bible study, and went to all the conferences. My dad always talked about how my mom was always in church. Then again, he was always there with her as well. There were times when my mom and dad were not treated fairly. I did not like seeing my parents mistreated. Even though it bothered me, there was a peace and contentment in them that only God could give. My mom held on to the Scriptures, and Philippians 4:4-9 (KJV) reminds me of her. *"Rejoice in the Lord always: and again, I say, Rejoice. Let your moderation be known unto all men. The Lord is at hand. Be careful for nothing; but in every thing by prayer and supplication with thanksgiving let your requests be made known unto God. And the peace of God, which passeth all understanding, shall keep your hearts and minds through Christ Jesus. Finally, brethren, whatsoever things are true, whatsoever things are honest, whatsoever things are just, whatsoever things are pure, whatsoever things are lovely, whatsoever things are of good report; if there be any virtue, and if there be any praise, think on these things. Those things, which ye have both learned, and received, and heard, and seen in me, do: and the God of peace shall be with you."*

My mom now suffers from Alzheimer's disease, and I am losing a piece of her each day. However, her faith in God has not changed. She does not remember much, but she still says, *"May God be with you."* I learned to hold on to the memories and thank God for them. This is a very difficult thing to go through. Watching my mom and realizing she is not the same person she was years ago is tough. I am grateful to still have her here with me. She said to me that I am the mama now. I am not sure what lesson I am learning through this situation, but God knows.

I am so thankful for all the lessons I have learned over the years. I realized God allowed things to happen to make me stronger. He is in control of my life and future. The things that we go through are just a season, not a sentence. It is temporary and not eternal. There is always hope. Romans 8:24-25 (NKJV) says, *"…But hope that is seen is not hope; for why does one still hope for what he sees? But if we hope for what we do not see, we eagerly wait for it with perseverance."* We are not victims of our circumstances and we must not live as though we are. That is when our faith is being tested. The greater the breakthrough, the greater the test. We are children of the Most High God.

Proverbs 1:5 says, *"A wise man will hear, and will increase learning; and a man of understanding shall attain unto wise counsels."*

Father, thank you for giving me gifts, talents and abilities to use in ministry to bless others as I give all Honor and Glory to you. I know that without the power and guidance of the Holy Spirit, I cannot accomplish anything. I pray for the Holy Spirit within me, to empower me so that I can use these gifts to empower your people, and that I reflect the character and compassion of Jesus, in whose name I pray. Amen.

CHAPTER 8
THE DAY MY LIFE CHANGED FOREVER

Even in the pain, I know there is a lesson and a plan.

Jeremiah 29:11 (NIV) "For I know the plans I have for you," declares the LORD, "plans to prosper you and not to harm you, plans to give you hope and a future.

This is one of my favorite Scriptures, and this year it just keeps coming before me in everything that I am experiencing and going through. It seems like every time I read a devotional, a book, or hear someone speak, there it Is. I am still not sure what it truly means to me at this time, but I have to trust and believe that God has a plan.

Let me explain what I mean and what I am going through. December 2024, Jeremiah 29:11 was deep in my spirit. I read it, studied it, and meditated on it. At the beginning of 2025, I spoke on it. For me, it was about grace. God had put this on my heart and in my spirit. When I thought about moving into a season of grace, I was thinking about our spiritual growth, our hope, our future. I realized that it is important - now more than ever - to focus on God. So many people I know are fearful and stressed. Mental health issues are at an all-time high. And if Christians lose sight of grace, they become irresponsible with the life God has given. We are distracted with all that is going on in our country and right in our own city. And, we are afraid to be honest with each other about how we really feel or what we are going through. Some of us are going things we have never experienced in our lifetime. It all seems unreal and too much for us to handle. This Scripture hits differently than what I had originally thought. My own life has changed drastically, and my future is a bit different now. But, I still choose to have hope.

My son passed away unexpectedly in 2025. I was totally devastated, and I will never be the same. In the midst of dealing with his passing, some other unfortunate things happened in my life that I need to grasp and understand before I can speak about them. Of course, my mom is still a priority, and life is still going forward. To get through these uncertain days as difficult as they are, I know I need to continue to trust in the LORD. Proverbs 3:5-6 (NKJV) says, "Trust in the Lord with all your heart, and lean not on your own understanding; In all your ways acknowledge Him, And He shall direct your paths."

This story began for me at the end of February when I returned from vacation and found out my son was not feeling well. I talked to him, and he said he had a cold, his stomach had not been right, and he could not eat. Of course, as Momma I asked all the questions, *"Have you been to the doctor?" "What are taking?" "Are you going to the bathroom?"* etc. He assured me it was just a cold, but he took time off from work, which is something he did not do.

My daughter said he had been dealing with issues for a while, so she went to his home and took him to the hospital where she works as a nurse. Well, they ran tests and found there was more going on than a cold. I was on the phone with him while he was in the emergency room and heard them talking or debating if they should tell me what was going on. They were concerned about me and did not want me to worry. I heard Michael say, "You know we have to tell her because she will investigate. She will ask a thousand questions and find out whatever is going on." Those two were always trying to keep things from me. Well, they told me what was going on but convinced me it wasn't too bad. They had to give him three pints of blood that night, and he stayed in the ER all night. My daughter was on duty, so she was able to keep an eye on him.

When I talked to him the next day, he told me how proud he was of his sister as he watched her do her job. He was amazed at how she handled patients and actually helped save lives. Now as I write this, I am thankful he got a chance to witness that because he was so excited about watching his sister work. He had a new respect for her profession. He mentioned it a couple of times that day as I talked to him. As their mom, it did my heart good. Once he was in a room, I went to the hospital to be with him. We talked about what was going on, and he was very optimistic. So was I.

Michael was a very private person, and he told us that he did not want any visitors except us. We respected that. I would go visit him, and he would send me home because I would stay late. He was concerned about me leaving at night. After a few days, I questioned why he was still in the hospital and was told that they were waiting on pathology. I made sure I stayed in contact with his job, as they seemed very concerned. They recognized how he did not normally take time off, so this was unusual. I was praying much for him. He was my baby, a grown man now with his own children, but at this time, he was my baby boy again.

When I would call him, I noticed he would be sleeping more. He said at one point, *"Mommy, you and Odaysia keep checking on me, but I'm okay. I'm just resting and sleeping."* One time when I was there, he shared with me the information he received about treatments, and we went over the options, the centers, and everything. He was still very optimistic, and so was I. I felt there was hope.

The next week on a Tuesday, Michael called me and wanted me to bring him some Coca-Cola – the real one. *"What do you mean?"* I inquired. He said his sister brought him some, but it was not the original. He gave me specific instructions: the original size, red can, no bottles or mini cans from the USA. I went to the store, and they only had the 12 pack, so that is what I bought. My son was pleased. He felt that it had some medicinal purpose for him.

As the days went on, the hospital gave him oxygen because his breathing was a little labored. This one particular day, Michael told me to sit on the bed with him, so I did. We talked about his children. I brought him pictures of his granddaughters in Florida. I had just returned a couple of weeks prior. I called his oldest son, Kai'im, and he talked to him and the girls. He said his grandchildren keep him going, and he wanted to see them again.

I questioned why he did not eat the food on his tray, and he informed me that he did eat the vegetables and the fruit, but that is all he would eat. He said he only wanted natural foods from the ground and commenced telling me how to eat. Always giving me instructions. We laughed so much that day. I told him how I felt about things, and he did the same. Michael had his own way of living, and I had mine, but we respected each other. He jokingly said, *"Ma, I always say what I want to say and talk smack to you, and you always come back with, 'Boy shut up! You're going to do what you want to do anyway.' I love you, Ma!"* We both acknowledged it was getting late. Before I left, I made sure he was comfortable, told him I loved him, and gave him a hug. He said, *"I love you too, Ma."*

The next day, Odaysia and her husband, Ben, were visiting Michael. I talked to Odaysia on the phone, and she said he was sleeping more, and his breathing was a little more labored. She said she would be there for a while, before going to work later. We always took turns being with him. He would always tell me we were bothering him while he tried to sleep, so because he seemed to be more comfortable in the morning, I would go visit him then.

That whole day I felt *off.* I was restless and could not quite get anything right. I needed to rest because I had not been able to sleep well, but I could not. Anyway, later that night I was feeling so anxious and could not sleep, so I had my husband stay up and watch movies with me, which was unusual for him because he is normally asleep while I am up watching television.

At 2 a.m., my phone rang. It was my daughter, who urged me to get to the hospital. I jumped up and left the house. When I got to the hospital, the security guys knew who I was and where I needed to go. They told me to go to the Intensive Care Unit. When I got there, Odaysia, Ben, and a nurse were sitting in the waiting room. Ironically, the nurse who was with her was the nurse who took care of Cameron, Odaysia's son, who passed away. And Odaysia took care of her mom in oncology. Now here she was with us once again. What a cycle! Odaysia proceeded to tell me they had called a code blue, which means a heart stoppage or life-threatening respiratory event in the hospital. She was working with a patient when the announcement first came in. When they announced it again, she realized it was her brother's room. The doctor who was with her told her to go. She then realized the hospital staff was also trying to call her.

Michael had gone into cardiac arrest. The nightmare had begun. We sat in the waiting room for what seemed like hours waiting for someone to come out to talk to us, although it really was not hours. My mind was all over the place. We talked about how Michael had progressed so fast. He had stopped breathing, and they had to put him on a ventilator. The whole time I was praying and hoping.

When the doctor came out to talk to us, I did not know what to expect. He told us that his kidneys were shutting down. He said they could start dialysis, but honestly, it would not do any good. The cancer in his body was spreading quickly. We went in to see him, and my heart just dropped. We were told to call our family because he would not make it through the morning. I could not believe what was happening. I called my husband, my siblings, and Michael's children. We were all with him praying and hoping this was a nightmare and not reality. We all came together around his bed, and I held his hand as he took his last breath. That was the most horrible feeling I have ever experienced in my life.

In the beginning, when you first lose a loved one, people are there. And it is appreciated and definitely needed. They are there to console you and do what is needed for the homegoing celebration. It was a blessing and a comfort.

For me, true love was shown and shared beyond what I expected when my Michael passed away. I was overwhelmed by the outpouring of all the flowers, cards, food, phone calls, and everything else provided to our family during that time. Kindness came not only from people we knew, but from those who we did not know. My house was full of flowers from the living room to the kitchen. It smelled like a florist shop when you walked through the door. Honestly, I felt like I was in the middle of a non-ending dream, or rather, a nightmare. I could not sleep nor eat. I could not grasp what I was going through. And for me, I could not talk to my mom to be comforted or held by her. She is suffering with

Alzheimer's, so she did not even know what was going on. My heart was broken, and I was hurting but could not go to my mom. She helped raise Michael, and that was her baby. I had to look at it as a blessing that she did not know what was going on so that she would not hurt as I was.

Together, my mother and I had gone through the passing of my nine-year-old grandson, my dad, and my brother, which were all very devastating for us both. When my grandson passed, she was there with my daughter and me. Her strength gave us strength, although our hearts were broken. It was one of the hardest deaths we experienced. I found myself not only grieving for Cameron, but also hurting for my daughter because of the pain she was dealing with. To watch your child go through this is one of the hardest things for a mom, and you cannot fully understand what it means to lose your child unless you have experienced it. For me, he was my grandchild; a part of me, but a more intimate part of my daughter who carried him for nine months. But because of the relationship, it all had me working hard not to get back into a depressed state.

For my mom, there was my dad, the man she had been married to for 57 years until his death. Then there was my brother, who was always there for her; her oldest son who passed away from cancer six and half months after my dad. I watched my mom go through both of these deaths, and it tore her apart. She became weaker. This all broke her. I watched my mom hurt, and I could not help her.

I learned that grief is a lonely road even when people are there for you. It is your journey alone because only you know what you are going through. Each person is different. Each death is different. It was hard for me when my brother passed away because we were very close and shared things that our other siblings did not. Although we handled situations differently, we had a bond that could not be broken. In the hospital he said, *"It's always going to be me and you, Sis."* One day while we were with him at the hospital during those last days, he yelled out while under medication, *"Debra and Jeff, let me go."* Jeff is our cousin who grew up with us. I had to assure him it was okay. And soon, he was gone. That was painful, and the hurt I felt from losing my brother was a bit much! So, I have a lot of personal pain from losing some of the closest males in my immediate family.

Now, here I am again. This time, I am the mother, and I now understand the pain my daughter and mom felt. If you have ever gone through this, you are mentally all over the place. That was a child you carried for nine months. The baby who you loved more than you loved yourself was a part of you most intimately. You watched him grow, cared for him, and ensured he had everything he needed to survive. I was there when my son took his first breath, and now I was there when he took his last breath. It was full circle for me, a circle that no parent should have to experience. Although my son was grown, he was still my baby, and I was his mom. We did not always see eye-to-eye, but what parent and child does.

As I share what I am going through at this moment and how I am feeling, it is very hard to explain the unexplainable. One moment I can be okay, and the next, I am crying, sad, or even angry. My mind is all over the place, and I cannot think straight half the time. Some days, it is hard to get out of bed. It is hard to tell people how I feel because, frankly, they do not really want to hear the truth. I just say, *"I'm okay."* and move on, even though I am not. How could I be? Most people mean well, but I have learned the hard way that you cannot understand what a person is really going through unless you have sat where they now sit.

I thought about a Scripture I read in the third chapter of Ezekiel. It came back to me because it helped me realize that I cannot blame people for not understanding my pain unless they have been there. God allowed me to be in the midst of some ladies who had been where I am, and I saw how they got strength from each other. It is not easy, and they acknowledged how difficult the days can be, even with encouragement from each other. Some have lost their children years ago, but it seems like it was just yesterday some days. I believe in God and trust Him, but the human part of me still cannot believe my son is gone.

Those days leading up to the funeral were almost a blur because we were so busy getting the service together. There was so much to do. We had a lot of help, and I am most grateful and thankful. One thing that really touched my heart that day was a big surprise from my son's job. When I walked into the church, the security guards and supervisors were lined up in the hallway to greet me. There had to be over 30 of them. I am so thankful for the outpouring of love shown for my son. He was not even a security guard at his job. He worked in the kitchen. His supervisor and a coworker spoke at the service.

The support from his job was so overwhelming, and it spoke volumes of the impact my son had made at the county jail. My family and friends were there supporting us, and I am thankful for everyone who took part in the service, although I really cannot tell you much about it. I was too grief-stricken. I do have a recording of it that I can watch…when I am ready.

Once the planning, service, burial, and repast are over, the crowds are gone and people go on with their lives. That is when reality sets in. People told me to call them if I needed them, and I truthfully said, *"I'm not going to call you. Know that we are not going to reach out for help."* Some have checked on me. Others have not, but I learned that it is okay. At first, I was trying to go on with my life, but then I realized my life was not the same. My normal had changed. Some people called it a *new normal*. It is definitely new. My only son was now gone. No more calls, texts, hugs, kisses, or deep debates between us. No more calls telling me what he wants me to cook for him and what I should not be eating. No more hearing his voice or seeing his face except in pictures, pictures that sometimes are hard to look at without breaking down. The first few months for me had been very difficult. I do not know how to give myself grace. I know it is going to take time. I am trying to continue with obligations and commitments that I had. Still smiling, being cordial and acting like the person I was, but struggling inside. This is a hard, lonely road for a mom. I learned that firsthand. People who have not experienced this really do not understand, and I did not either until now. Right now, there is a sadness that I cannot get rid of inside of me, even when I am smiling. I am grateful for my family who are here, but I miss the one who first called me Mom.

I cherish the memories and, of course, there are some things I wish I had done differently. I am sure all parents go through that part, even with their living children. I think of my son all the time, sometimes in tears and sometimes with a smile. I am not sure how to get through the days ahead and the nights that seem even harder. But as I go through, I am grateful to God who gives me a peace that surpasses all understanding, because I cannot understand how I am still standing. I am thankful for those who are closest to me who think it not robbery to check on me, get me out of the house, and just show love, even though they do not always know where my head is at any given moment. My emotions are all over the place, and my family have been patient with me. That is a real blessing.

So, now you know my story, but this is not the end. I know God is continuing to work in my life. I do not know why this happened at this time, and I do not know what God has in store for me in the future, but I know He has a plan. I have to trust Him with everything in me, although this has caused me great pain. I know I am imperfect, but perfectly made by God. Even in the pain, I know there is a lesson. My son is at peace. No suffering. No more pain.

I need to rest and restore my spirit. I need that deeper healing right now that I cannot get on my own. If you are in a state of grief, tribulation, or mental anguish, please understand that only Jesus can bring you that kind of healing. Go to Him as often as it takes for as long as it takes. Psalm 147:3 (NKJV) tells us, *"He heals the brokenhearted and binds up their wounds."* Let this be a reminder to everyone reading this today.

I am writing this in memory of you, Michael. I will always love and remember you. I will hold you deep in my heart, my firstborn baby.

CHAPTER 9
REFLECT

You are never too old to set another goal; dream a new dream; nor learn a new lesson! Everything may not work out at first but do not give up. My prayer, goal, and intention were to have my first book draft by the end of 2023, and that did not happen. However, with God, all things are possible in His timing. Just trust and believe.

Psalm 62:5-8 (NIV), *"Yes, my soul, find rest in God; my hope comes from him. Truly he is my rock and my salvation; he is my fortress, I will not be shaken. My salvation and my honor depend on God; he is my mighty rock, my refuge. Trust In him at all times, you people; pour out your hearts to him, for God is our refuge."*

A Letter to myself:

To the woman in the mirror,
You know that Jesus says, 'I am with you to the end of the earth'. You must remember you are wonderfully and fearfully made. You are beautiful and creative because you were created in God's image. You will dream dreams that will come true. Remember to trust in Jesus and allow His words to resonate in your spirit. Love the person you have become; a gifted writer and teacher. Believe you will transform lives without even knowing the length and breadth of your influence in this world.

Loving who I am,
Always me

Reflect: Trusting God means we will give up worrying, self-reasoning and anxiety. We must have the faith of a child, believing that God has our best interest at heart. We must trust and believe that Jesus, with the help of the Holy Spirit, will guide us and lead us into peace with God and will help us do what we cannot do alone. This is a process and will not happen overnight. We must take one day at a time.

Ask yourself:

- What am I believing God for?
- What do I need to let go of or change in my life to enter into the peace and rest God has for me?
- How do I trust in God and give my life over to Him completely?
- What does it mean to have inner peace?

ACKNOWLEDGMENTS

I must acknowledge and thank the ladies who made sure I stayed on track, my writing group: Dr. Deborah Nazon PhD, Jessica Otitigbe, Michandra Lindsey, and Taunya Williams Esq, who listened to me, supported me, and always encouraged me through this project when I needed it. These ladies rocked when it came to support.

Thanks to three other special people on my journey: Honorable Sharon Bowles, Esq., the Rev. Dr. Damone P. Johnson, and the Rev. Dr. Edward O. Williamson for your assistance in this process.

To Lisa King DeJesus and the entire team at King Jesus Press, I am so grateful for your guidance through this process. I take none of you for granted, and I thank God for you all!

ABOUT THE AUTHOR

Mrs. Debra A. Williams truly loves the LORD. She has a passion for Christian Education and loves teaching, mentoring, sharing encouraging words, and is a continuous learner. Her church, local association, and community involvement - as well as her leadership skills (evidenced by her works) - is a testament of the woman of God she is. She serves faithfully in her church, Shiloh Baptist Church, Hudson NY, where her husband, Rev. Alan E. Williams serves as pastor.

Debra currently serves as the president of the Golconda Council of Baptist Ministers' Wives and Widows, and registrar and assistant dean of the Empire Baptist Missionary Convention (EBMC) Congress of Christian Education. She previously served as president of the Congress of Christian Education; Hudson River Frontier Missionary Baptist Association (HRFMBA). She was the first female/layperson to serve in that capacity. She has also served in many capacities in Sunday School/B.T.U. including secretary and vice president, and director of Christian education and the HRFMBA Christian Leadership School. She has also taught at several local churches over the years.

Debra has been teaching in the EBMC Congress of Christian Education One Day Retreat (Intermediate Department) since 1998. Before that, she taught in the Ministers' Wives Division. Debra has been teaching in the weeklong EBMC Congress of Christian Education since 1999 and is certified to teach several classes. She had an article published in "Theology Digest," "Persecution and the Spread of Christianity" in 2008 and an article published in the Adult Study Guide on Discipleship (EBMC Congress) in 2017.

In the community, Debra has volunteered and taught weekly Bible Study at Homer Perkins Drug and Rehab Center, volunteered at Mercy House (a home for women at risk), was previously on the Board of Directors at Drake Manor (Senior Housing) and has served as secretary. She has volunteered with Make a Wish Foundation and the Community Hospice where she has participated in the Walk for Hospice for more than 12 years. Debra continues to raise funds for the organization. She received the President's medal of Honor under President George

W. Bush for sending spiritual encouragement to troops in Afghanistan.

As much as Debra loves to teach, she also loves to learn. Some of her academic accomplishments include Business Administration at Albany Business College, Bachelor of Theology at O.M. Kelly Religious Training Institute, paralegal studies, graduated Suma Cum Laude with a 4.0 GPA from Bryant & Stratton College, inducted into Alpha Beta Kappa National Honor Society, taken several classes through CLS and the EMBC Congress of Christian Education, and received a 98.9 in Black Theology from New Life School of Theology. Debra is also a certified dean through the Sunday School Publishing Board, NBC. She also graduated Magna Cum Laude from the Rawlings Theological Seminary at Liberty University with her B.S. Degree in Biblical & Educational Studies (C.E.) with a 3.60 GPA.

Debra retired from Verizon Communications after 40 years of service. Her real comfort and joy is her family. She is the wife of the Rev. Alan E. Williams; daughter of Virginia Watson; mother of Michael, Marcus, and Odaysia; grandmother of seven; and great grandmother of five.